MIGHTY MACHINES IN ACTION

Big Rigs

by Rebecca Pettiford

BELLWETHER MEDIA • MINNEAPOLIS, MN

Note to Librarians, Teachers, and Parents:

Blastoff! Readers are carefully developed by literacy experts and combine standards-based content with developmentally appropriate text.

Level 1 provides the most support through repetition of high-frequency words, light text, predictable sentence patterns, and strong visual support.

Level 2 offers early readers a bit more challenge through varied simple sentences, increased text load, and less repetition of high-frequency words.

Level 3 advances early-fluent readers toward fluency through increased text and concept load, less reliance on visuals, longer sentences, and more literary language.

Level 4 builds reading stamina by providing more text per page, increased use of punctuation, greater variation in sentence patterns, and increasingly challenging vocabulary.

Level 5 encourages children to move from "learning to read" to "reading to learn" by providing even more text, varied writing styles, and less familiar topics.

Whichever book is right for your reader, Blastoff! Readers are the perfect books to build confidence and encourage a love of reading that will last a lifetime!

This edition first published in 2018 by Bellwether Media, Inc.

No part of this publication may be reproduced in whole or in part without written permission of the publisher. For information regarding permission, write to Bellwether Media, Inc., Attention: Permissions Department, 5357 Penn Avenue South, Minneapolis, MN 55419.

Library of Congress Cataloging-in-Publication Data

Names: Pettiford, Rebecca, author.
Title: Big Rigs / by Rebecca Pettiford.
Description: Minneapolis, MN : Bellwether Media, Inc., [2018] | Series: Blastoff! Readers. Mighty Machines in Action | Includes bibliographical references and index. | Audience: Grades K-3. | Audience: Ages 5-8.
Identifiers: LCCN 2016052751 (print) | LCCN 2016055666 (ebook) | ISBN 9781626176294 (hardcover : alk. paper) | ISBN 9781681033594 (ebook)
Subjects: LCSH: Tractor trailer combinations–Juvenile literature. | Trucks–Juvenile literature.
Classification: LCC TL230.15 .P477 2018 (print) | LCC TL230.15 (ebook) | DDC 629.224–dc23
LC record available at https://lccn.loc.gov/2016052751

Editor: Christina Leighton   Designer: Steve Porter

Printed in the United States of America, North Mankato, MN.

Table of Contents

BIG TRUCKS

Roar! A big rig thunders down the road. It arrives at a store.

docks

The driver slowly backs the truck into a **dock**.

trailer

Workers open the truck's **trailer**. They unload many boxes.

Soon, the big rig drives off to pick up another load!

HEAVY LOADS

OVERSIZE LOAD

Big rigs are also called
tractor-trailers and semis.

They **transport** heavy loads in all kinds of weather.

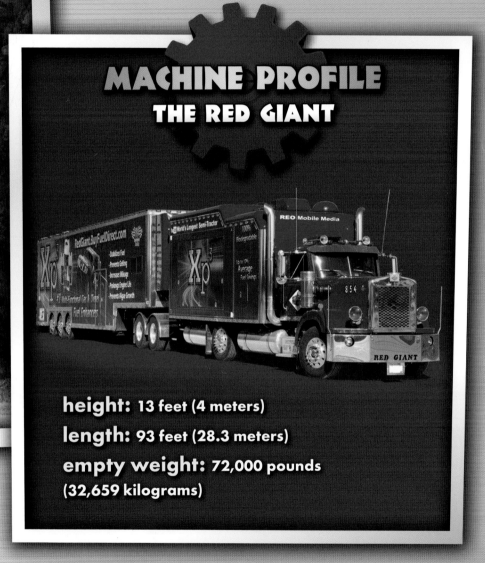

MACHINE PROFILE
THE RED GIANT

height: 13 feet (4 meters)

length: 93 feet (28.3 meters)

empty weight: 72,000 pounds (32,659 kilograms)

Many big rigs carry **containers**. Some move liquids in **tanks**.

BIG RIG SIZE

height: 13.5 feet (4.1 meters)

average human

length: 75 feet (23 meters)

flatbed

Others transport wood and
building materials on **flatbeds**.

TRACTORS, TRAILERS, AND WHEELS

The front part of a big rig is the **tractor**. The driver sits in the tractor's **cab**.

tractor

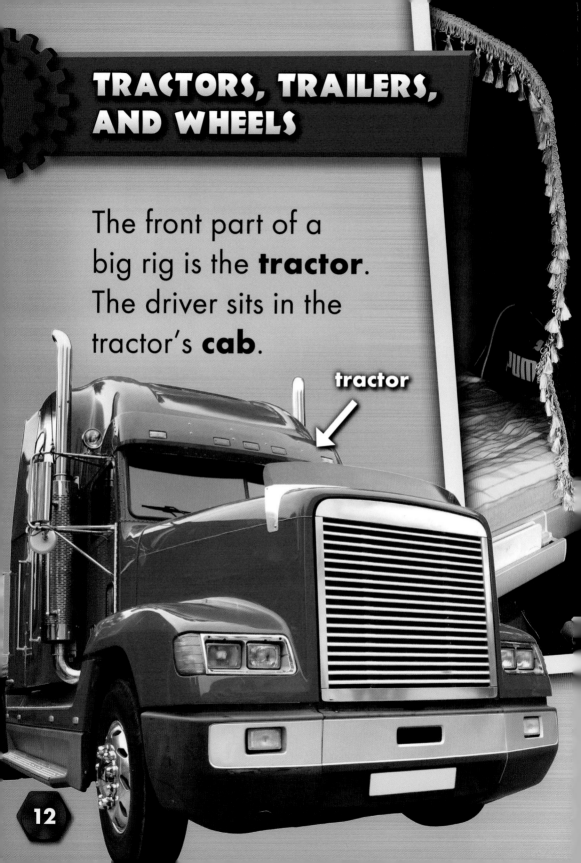

cab

Some cabs are big enough for a bed and small refrigerator!

The back part of a big rig is called the trailer. This carries the **cargo**.

trailer

fifth wheel

A **fifth wheel** attaches the trailer to the tractor.

Many big rigs have 18 wheels to carry the heavy cargo.

The machines need a lot of
room to stop. Their brakes fill
with air and then release it.

Big rigs need powerful engines
to pull cargo.

These engines use a lot of **diesel fuel**. They are loud!

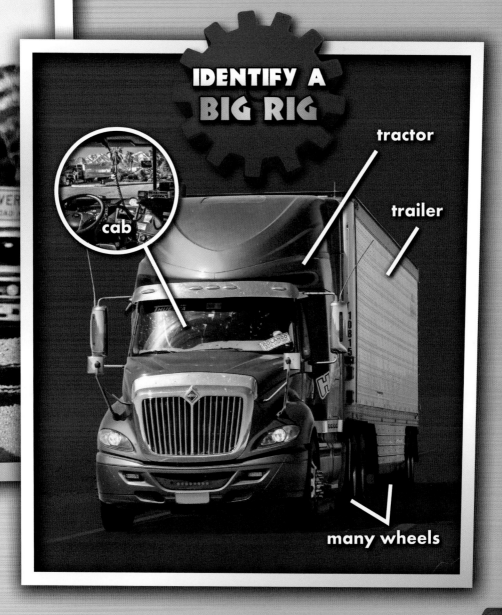

IDENTIFY A
BIG RIG

tractor

trailer

cab

many wheels

Big rigs travel near and far to bring goods from place to place.

No matter where they go,
big rigs work hard!

Glossary

cab—the part of a big rig where the driver sits

cargo—something that is carried by a big rig

containers—large boxes that hold goods

diesel fuel—a type of oil that is burned in diesel engines

dock—a place where materials are loaded and unloaded

fifth wheel—a large, circular part on a big rig that holds the tractor and trailer together

flatbeds—trailers that have bodies that are flat or shaped like shallow boxes

tanks—containers that hold liquids

tractor—a powerful machine that pulls or carries equipment

trailer—the back part of a big rig that carries loads

transport—to carry from place to place

To Learn More

AT THE LIBRARY

Arnold, Quinn M. *Big Rigs*. Mankato, Minn.:
Creative Education, 2017.

Silverman, Buffy. *How Do Big Rigs Work?*
Minneapolis, Minn.: Lerner Publications, 2016.

Spaight, Anne J. *Big Rigs on the Go.* Minneapolis,
Minn.: Lerner Publications, 2017.

ON THE WEB

Learning more about big rigs
is as easy as 1, 2, 3.

1. Go to www.factsurfer.com.

2. Enter "big rigs" into the search box.

3. Click the "Surf" button and you will see a
list of related web sites.

With factsurfer.com, finding more
information is just a click away.

Index